Read & Respond

FOR
KS1

Read & Respond

FOR KS1

Author: Jean Evans

Development Editor: Simret Brar

Editor: Alex Albrighton

Assitant Editor: Pam Kelt

Series Designer: Anna Oliwa

Designer: Liz Gilbert

Illustrations: Simon James and Theresa Tibbetts/Beehive Illustration

Text © 2009, Jean Evans © 2009 Scholastic Ltd

Designed using Adobe InDesign

Published by Scholastic Ltd, Villiers House,
Clarendon Avenue, Leamington Spa,
Warwickshire CV32 5PR
www.scholastic.co.uk

Printed by Bell & Bain
1 2 3 4 5 6 7 8 9   9 0 1 2 3 4 5 6 7 8

British Library Cataloguing-in-Publication Data
A catalogue record for this book is available from the
British Library.
ISBN 978-1407-11395-1

Acknowledgements
The publishers gratefully acknowledge permission to reproduce the following copyright material: **Walker Books Ltd** for the use of text and illustrations from *Dear Greenpeace* by Simon James © 1991, Simon James (1991, Walker Books). Every effort has been made to trace copyright holders for the works reproduced in this book, and the publishers apologise for any inadvertent omissions.

Dear Greenpeace

About the book

Dear Greenpeace is a delightful story featuring an imaginative girl called Emily who finds a whale in her garden pond. Worried that he might be unhappy, she writes to Greenpeace for advice. Greenpeace tries to be helpful, but informs her that whales do not live in garden ponds, as they prefer salt water. Emily tries adding salt to the water in the pond and, with determination, continues to write further letters asking questions about the whale she is becoming increasingly fond of.

The author uses a definite format, with consistent variation of language to determine who is writing and receiving the letters, and the purpose behind them. There is a marked contrast between the caring informal letters from Emily about her whale, known to her as Arthur, and the formal factual responses of Greenpeace. As the book progresses, Emily is saddened by the disappearance of Arthur and receives a sympathetic response from Greenpeace. However, the story draws to a satisfactory conclusion when Emily finds Arthur at the seaside where he lets her stroke his head and she shares her sandwich with him.

Although set in the familiar surroundings of Emily's home, *Dear Greenpeace*, is an example of a fantasy story with a strong ecological message. Children will sympathise with Emily over her dilemma and her desire to make her whale happy. Their understanding of the main character, particularly the strength of her imagination and determination, can be developed through drama and role play. As they take part, their own appreciation of the differences between reality and fantasy will be enhanced.

Shared reading of the text provides excellent opportunities for teaching and applying Key Stage 1 word level skills, and for developing children's understanding of sentence construction and punctuation. The book is an ideal starting point to motivate children into their own research relating to environmental issues, and endangered species in particular.

About the author

Simon James grew up in Bristol and Exeter and spent much of his childhood drawing and writing stories which he made into little books. He was fascinated by his father's books 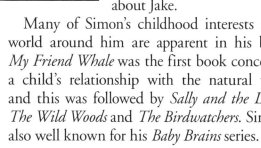 on cartoonists and tried to copy some of them. He was also interested in ecological issues from a young age and spent his time climbing trees and trying to save worms from puddles.

Simon studied graphic design and art history at college and this helped him to understand the techniques used in creating picture books. His first book, published in 1989, was *The Day Jake Vacuumed*, and this was followed by soon after by two more books about Jake.

Many of Simon's childhood interests in the world around him are apparent in his books. *My Friend Whale* was the first book concerning a child's relationship with the natural world, and this was followed by *Sally and the Limpet, The Wild Woods* and *The Birdwatchers*. Simon is also well known for his *Baby Brains* series.

Facts and figures

Simon James is one of the country's leading author/illustrators. His books have won several awards:
• *Leon and Bob* won the Smarties Book Prize Silver Award and was the *New York Times'* Best Illustrated Book of the Year
• *Days Like This*, a collection of small poems, was shortlisted for the Kate Greenaway Medal
• *Baby Brains* was the overall winner of the Red House Children's Book Award in 2005, voted for by 25,000 children, and has been translated into 15 languages.

Guided reading

Introducing the book

Introduce the book and refer to the title, cover, pages, illustrations and blurb to make predictions about the story.

Begin by exploring the illustration on the front cover together. Look at the image of the stamp and ask the children to describe it. Ask: *Who is the girl on the stamp? What is she doing? Who do you think she is writing to? What time of day is it?* Draw the children's attention to the red lines beside the stamp and ask them what this might be. (A postmark.) Have some letters to hand so that the children can pass them around and find the postmarks. Ask: *Does this postmark tell us where the writer of the letter posted it?* (Plymouth.) Look up Plymouth on a map and establish that it is by the sea.

Read the title together. Ask: *Does the title tell us what the story might be about? Who might Greenpeace be?* Draw attention to the smaller print underneath it and read the words together. Ask: *Do these words tell us more about the story?* (There is a whale in Emily's pond.) *Can you guess who Emily might be?* (The girl on the stamp.)

Draw the children's attention to the author's name, Simon James. Encourage them to name the authors of some of their favourite books. Explain that Simon James is also the illustrator of this book and discuss the work of an illustrator. To extend this discussion, and find out more about some of the books Simon James has written, turn to the last page of *Dear Greenpeace* or visit the publisher's website, www.walker.co.uk. (There is also some information about Simon James on page 3 of this book.)

Turn to the back cover and read the invitation by Emily to read the book. In the light of this invitation, and the words on the front cover, encourage children to comment again about the content of the story.

Initial reading

The first time that you share *Dear Greenpeace* with the children, focus on making the experience enjoyable. Read the story clearly and expressively,

encouraging the children to participate by joining in, asking questions or listening with interest. Modify your voice to differentiate between the two letter writers, Emily and Greenpeace. Indicate words by moving along them with a finger or pointer as you read, and remember to pause at significant points to ask children what they think will happen next or to predict a word or phrase. Ask, for example: *What do you think Emily will do now that Greenpeace has given this advice? How do you think Greenpeace will answer Emily's question about what to feed her whale?*

As you continue to read, ensure that the children understand the text through appropriate comments and queries, such as: *What did Greenpeace tell Emily about creatures that are migratory?* Give an example from the children's experience to clarify this point – for instance, talk about birds in their gardens flying to warmer lands in the winter.

Encourage the children to empathise with Emily by making links with their experiences. Ask questions such as: *Have you ever felt sad or lost something you really liked? Can you say when? Have people ever ignored you? What did you do to make yourself feel better?* Try to encourage them to understand how their own experiences help them to 'feel' the emotions of the characters when they are reading a story.

Always be prepared to follow the children's comments, interests and ideas when they talk about how they would react in similar situations. Draw attention to and emphasise the importance of illustrations in enhancing the story.

Finally, encourage the children to share their initial opinions. Ask: *Did you enjoy the book? What did you like about it? Was there anything you did not like? Do you think that telling the story through letters works?*

Subsequent readings

Once the children are familiar with the book, and have shared the enjoyment of a first reading, plan further readings carefully to focus on different aspects to extend children's comprehension of

Guided reading

the text, develop fluency in reading aloud and increase their word and sentence level objectives.

The children should be taught to:
- use a range of decoding strategies for unfamiliar words, check for meaning and self-correct errors
- build up words and understand spelling patterns in context
- read high frequency words on sight
- develop understanding of sentence construction and punctuation
- read aloud with pace and expression appropriate to the grammar of the text
- track the text from left to right and word by word
- understand and use book- and print-related terms correctly
- identify story elements (plot, character, setting)
- predict and infer
- sequence story events.

Setting the scene

Ask the children to read the first letter from Emily and the reply from Greenpeace. Encourage them to use a combination of phonic knowledge, picture cues along with re-reading of sentences to do so.

Pose questions to help them determine how this section of the book sets the scene for the story: *What does Emily feel about whales?* (She loves them very much.) *Why did she write to Greenpeace for information when she saw a whale in her pond?* (She thought it might be hurt.) *What do we discover from the reply from Greenpeace?* (Greenpeace did not believe Emily because whales live in salt water.)

Invite the children to discuss how the story progresses from this point – for example, by talking about how Emily uses the information about salt water. Extend this discussion with ideas about how the story could develop in different ways. Ask: *Emily continues to help her whale by writing to Greenpeace with questions she needs answering, but what could have happened instead?*

Blue whales

Continue to read the story, pausing to focus on Emily's letter beginning *Tonight I am very happy...* Ask: *What two questions does Emily ask in her letter?* (*Does this mean he might be a blue whale? What can I feed him with?*) *How can we tell they are questions?* (There is a question mark at the end of each sentence.)

Make a list of blue whale facts given in the next two responses from Greenpeace. (They are blue, eat shrimp-like creatures, live in the sea, are migratory and are too big to live in ponds.) Point out the question asked by Greenpeace at the bottom of the letter: *Perhaps it is a blue goldfish?* Explain that the letters 'P.S.' (post scriptum) mean that Greenpeace thought about this after the letter was written and added this question at the end.

Exploring a letter from Emily

Read Emily's letter beginning *Last night I read your letter...* and explore how the words and punctuation chosen by the author show Emily's feelings and actions.

Ask the children: *How was she feeling when she stroked the whale's head?* (Excited.) *How did she take the cornflakes and breadcrumbs to the whale?* (Secretly.) *Emily read the letter from Greenpeace to the whale and thought of a name for him – what does this tell us about how she felt towards him?* (She wanted to share things with him, she cared for him, he was her friend.) *What is the effect of the exclamation mark after the words ...all gone?* (Emily is surprised). *Does Emily ask any questions? How do you know?* (She asks, *I think I shall call him Arthur, what do you think?* There is a question mark at the end of the sentence.)

Real or imaginary?

Ask the children if they think the whale is real or in Emily's imagination. Read the words on the comments page stating that the book is 'a work of fiction'. Ask: *What does this tell*

Guided reading

us? (It might not all be true, the author might have imagined it some of it.) Ask the children to think of things that Emily might have seen that looked like a whale, such as a large fish or a dark shadow.

Explore the book for words that suggest that the whale is imaginary. (*I think I saw one, whales don't live in ponds, I saw my whale smile, there can't be a whale in your pond, a blue whale is much too big to live in your pond*, and *in no way could a whale live in your pond*.)

Book review

After discussing the story, characters and specific events in detail, invite the children to reconsider their initial impressions of the book through personal responses. Enlarge upon your original questions and give positive encouragement to help them to voice their opinions in more detail, and with confidence and clarity. Ask: *What was the story about? What was your favourite part of the story? Was there anything about it that you did not enjoy? Who is the main character? Is there anything that you particularly liked or disliked about her? Can you say why you feel like this? What do you think of the character of the whale? Do you think he is friendly or fierce? What makes you think this?*

Shared reading

Extract 1

● Display an enlarged copy of the extract, and read it aloud together. Encourage the children to use knowledge of high frequency words, recognise alternative ways of spelling graphemes already taught (such as *whales, today* and *might*) and decode more challenging words such as *information* and *Greenpeace*.
● Ask the children to identify the two sentences in the letter by circling the capital letter at the start and full-stop at the end of each one. Ask: *Can you find any other capital letters in the extract?*

Explain that capital letters are also used for names of people and organisations, and find the names *Emily* and *Greenpeace*.
● Cover the opening and closing words: *Dear Greenpeace* and *love Emily*. Invite the children to read the letter, predict the missing words and write them in. Split the word *Greenpeace* into *Green* and *peace* to support spelling.
● Explore the accompanying illustration and discuss how it links with, and adds detail to, the text.

Extract 2

● Display an enlarged copy of the extract and discuss why it is in italics. (All the Greenpeace letters are printed in this way in the book.) Read it together. Ask: *Who is the letter from? Which closing word tells us it is a formal letter?* (*Sincerely.*)
● Ask the children to find two words that sound the same but have different spellings. (*No* and *know.*) Discuss the meaning of each word in the context of the letter. Ask: *Can you think of another word that has the same meaning as 'know'?* (*Understand.*)
● Invite the children to find the long words in the extract – *forcefully, migratory, distances,*

disappoint, sincerely. Write the words on the whiteboard and challenge the children to read each one by breaking it down and applying their phonic knowledge and skills. Praise children for their efforts and offer support if any words prove too difficult fot them. Finally, read the words out loud in context to ensure the children's understanding.
● Explore the accompanying illustration and discuss how it extends the text information. (Emily is absorbing the information from Greenpeace on her way to school.)

Extract 3

● Display an enlarged copy of the extract and read it together. Discuss how the text indicates Emily's mood. Ask: *Do you think Emily was happy when she wrote this letter? Which words tell us this?* (*Happiest day* and the fact that Arthur *smiled.*) Talk about Emily's conversational way of writing to Greenpeace, indicated by the words *you'll never guess, I hope you don't mind* and *I said you loved him too.*
● Ask the children to find the exclamation marks in the extract. Explain that they demonstrate the depth of Emily's feelings and so the words preceding them should be read with emphasis. Invite children to read the sentences ending in

exclamation marks with this in mind.
● Explain that the dots after the word *sandwich* indicate that the reader should pause to increase the drama of the moment when Arthur and Emily say goodbye. Read this together, pausing appropriately to end the sentence with feeling.
● Point to the brackets enclosing the words *and Arthur* at the end of the letter and explain that this might indicate that Emily added his name as an afterthought. Talk about the meaning of the word *afterthought*.
● Explore the accompanying images with the class and discuss how they link with the text and extend the information.

Extract 1

Dear Greenpeace,
    I love whales very much and
I think I saw one in my pond
today. Please send me some
information on whales, as
I think he might be hurt.

        love
        Emily

Extract 2

Dear Emily,

I must point out to you quite forcefully now that in no way could a whale live in your pond. You may not know that whales are migratory, which means that they travel great distances each day.

I am sorry to disappoint you.

Yours sincerely,

Greenpeace

Extract 3

Dear Greenpeace,

It's been the happiest day!
I went to the seaside and you'll
never guess, but I saw Arthur!
I called to him and he smiled.
I knew it was Arthur because
he let me stroke his head.

I gave him some of my sandwich...
and then we said goodbye.

I shouted that I loved him very
much and, I hope you don't mind,
I said you loved him too.

love
Emily (and Arthur)

Text and illustration © 1991, Simon James.

SCHOLASTIC
www.scholastic.co.uk

Plot, character and setting

All about Emily

> **Objective:** To identify the main events and characters in stories, and find specific information in simple texts.
> **What you need:** Copies of *Dear Greenpeace* and photocopiable page 15.

What to do
● Read *Dear Greenpeace* with the class and talk about the main character, Emily. Initiate a discussion about the children's first impressions of Emily from just listening to the story.
● Discuss the role that Greenpeace plays. Ask: *Do you think people at Greenpeace can be called characters in the story? Can we say anything about them?*
● Invite the children to build up a character profile for Emily, explaining the meaning of *character* and *profile*. Refer to *Dear Greenpeace* for ideas and make a list of appropriate words,

such as *kind, caring, determined* and *loving*.
● Discuss whether the whale is real or just in Emily's imagination. Does this mean Emily is *observant* or very *imaginative*? Ask the children to justify their responses.
● Talk about how images help with character profiling – for example, Emily is pictured as *concentrating, thoughtful, sad* and *overjoyed*.
● During discussions, display an enlarged version of photocopiable page 15 so that children can write their suggested words in the boxes. Ensure that they understand how to fill in the sheet before giving a copy to each child to complete.

> **Differentiation**
> **For older/more confident learners:** Ask the children to write a profile of a family member or friend.
> **For younger/less confident learners:** Encourage the children to focus on the appearance of Emily by looking closely at the book's illustrations.

Emily's feelings

> **Objective:** To visualise and comment on events, characters and ideas, making imaginative links to their own experiences.
> **What you need:** Copies of *Dear Greenpeace* and photocopiable page 16.
> **Cross-curricular link:** PSHE.

What to do
● Read *Dear Greenpeace* and invite the children to look for evidence of Emily's family life. Draw attention to the family photograph on the stairs and ask who the people might be.
● Explore the illustration of baby at breakfast and images of Dad. Notice how he always appears in the background, reading a paper, watching TV or having a drink. Discuss how Emily seems isolated, despite her family's presence.
● Talk with the class about how Emily feels sorting the 'whale' problem out by herself. How do they think she feels when she is alone?

● Encourage the children to discuss their own feelings of isolation, focusing on instances of being alone or having a problem to solve.
● Display an enlarged copy of photocopiable page 16 and explore the book image of Emily on her bed. Invite children to suggest words to describe her feelings. Choose some of them to put in a sentence in the box underneath.
● Explain what the children need to do to complete the rest of the sheet, before giving a copy to each child to work on.

> **Differentiation**
> **For older/more confident learners:** Ask the children to draw a picture of a happy family event and to write a sentence about how they were feeling underneath.
> **For younger/less confident learners:** Encourage the children to draw a picture of their family and write the names of their family members under each person.

Plot, character and setting

The Greenpeace team

> **Objective:** To interpret a text by reading aloud with some variety in pace and emphasis.
> **What you need:** Copies of *Dear Greenpeace* letters and adult dressing-up clothes.
> **Cross-curricular link:** Drama.

What to do
● Before the lesson, explore the Greenpeace website (www.greenpeace.org.uk). Share sections with the children that explain its role and current projects. Ask: *Why did Emily write to Greenpeace? What kind of information did she ask for?*
● Talk about the different letter-writing styles in *Dear Greenpeace*. (Emily's informal letters and the formal letters from Greenpeace.) Discuss how we know whether the letters are from Emily or Greenpeace. (By the opening closing words and the complexity of language.) Experiment with voice variation to convey differences and emotions when reading the letters aloud – for example, when saying *forcefully, sincerely, love* and *Please don't be sad*. Consider how our voices change when we ask a question.
● Ask the children to work in groups of six. Five members of each group will take on the role of Greenpeace, sitting opposite the sixth member, who is Emily. Provide each Greenpeace representative with a copy of a laminated letter, in the order they appear in the book. Arrange Emily's letters in the correct order for reading.
● Invite the children to tell the story by reading the letters in order, starting with Emily's first letter. Remind them to put expression into their reading.

> **Differentiation**
> **For older/more confident learners:** Provide imaginary letter problems for the children to reply to – for example, *We would like to save energy in our classroom. Can you advise us what we can do?*
> **For younger/less confident learners:** Encourage the children to write letters by providing a designated office area for role play.

When I grow up

> **Objective:** To take turns to speak, listen to others' suggestions and talk about what they are going to do.
> **What you need:** *Dear Greenpeace* and enlarged and individual copies of photocopiable page 17.
> **Cross-curricular link:** PSHE.

What to do
● Read the letter from Greenpeace suggesting that Emily sails the oceans studying and protecting whales when she grows up.
● Look at the illustration depicting Emily deep in thought in her bedroom. Ask: *What do you think is in Emily's mind? What does the picture tell us about Emily's interests?* (Music, sailing, whales, animals.) *What occupations do you think Emily could do to link with these interests?* (Scientist, vet, explorer, wildlife park warden or sailor.) *Thinking about the rest of the story, what clues tell us about things that Emily likes to do at home?* (She reads books and writes letters.)
● Ask the children about their interests and what they would like to do when they grow up.
● Display the enlarged copy of photocopiable page 17 and read the questions together to stimulate ideas and discussion.
● Provide each child with a copy of the photocopiable sheet to complete and then bring the class together to discuss responses.

> **Differentiation**
> **For older/more confident learners:** Ask a child to pretend to be Emily while others ask about her interests and what she wants to be when she grows up.
> **For younger/less confident learners:** Encourage the children to draw a picture of what they would like to do when they grow up and help them to construct a sentence to write underneath.

Plot, character and setting

Book publishers

Objective: To ensure that everyone contributes and allocate tasks; to consider alternatives and reach agreement.
What you need: Copies of *Dear Greenpeace*, cameras, printing facilities, writing materials, paper, collage and recycled materials, photographic props such as curtains, dressing-up clothes, small bowl and a plastic whale.
Cross-curricular links: ICT, art.

What to do
● Read *Dear Greenpeace* and discuss the people involved in creating a book, such as the author, image creator (illustrator/photographer), editor and publisher. Allocate groups to these roles.
● Suggest making a class version of the story, using photographs instead of illustrations. Create a storyboard of images needed and discuss how to set up scenes to photograph – for example, Emily looking out of a curtained window at the whale. Suggest making props, such as a miniature pond from a bowl of water with green cellophane plants and a small plastic whale.
● Invite the image creators to set up and take the photographs. Involve all children in choosing which ones to print.
● Provide the authors with the chosen photographs to write sentences about.
● Pass the photographs and text to the editors to check that the words match the images.
● Present the publishers with the images and edited text to make into a book using large sheets of paper, staples and glue.

Differentiation
For older/more confident learners: Invite groups of children to create simple copies of other favourite stories in this way.
For younger/less confident learners: Encourage the children to dress up as story characters and pose for a photograph. Support them with writing a caption underneath their printed image.

Alternative endings

Objective: To adopt appropriate roles in small or large groups and consider alternative courses of action.
What you need: Copies of *Dear Greenpeace*.

What to do
● Read *Dear Greenpeace* and then focus on the final letter from Emily. Discuss how the author uses words effectively to draw the story to a satisfying conclusion – for example, *It's been the happiest day!* Talk about traditional endings, such as *They lived happily ever after*.
● Encourage imaginative language by asking the children to think of an alternative ending for the story. Stimulate ideas initially by introducing some different scenarios – for example, *What would happen if… Emily did not find Arthur? Emily's Dad had a large swimming pool built in the garden for Arthur? Emily's family decided to move to the seaside?*
● Discuss whether the ending should be happy or sad. Which do the children prefer and why?
● Invite the children to work in groups of four to discuss alternative story endings. Suggest that they take turns to scribe, noting down ideas and then creating sentences. When they have finished, ask them to choose a storyteller to read out their ending to the rest of the class.
● Bring the class together to hear the endings and decide which are most effective and why.

Differentiation
For older/more confident learners: Invite the children to write alternative endings to traditional stories, such as 'The Three Billy Goats Gruff' or 'Goldilocks and the Three Bears'.
For younger/less confident learners: Read stories with predictable happy endings, and encourage the children to join in so that they experience the satisfaction of traditional story language.

Plot, character and setting

Letter replies

> **Objective:** To maintain consistency in non-narrative, including purpose and tense.
> **What you need:** Copies of *Dear Greenpeace* and photocopiable page 18.

What to do
- Read out the letters in *Dear Greenpeace* in a random order and ask the children who wrote each one. How did they know? Discuss clues that help us to decide – for example, Emily finishes her letters with *Love Emily* rather than the more formal *Yours sincerely* from Greenpeace. Emily writes as she would talk and asks lots of questions. Greenpeace responds in a more practical way with facts and information because it is giving answers rather than asking questions.
- Display the enlarged copy of photocopiable page 18 and read the different letters together. Explain to the children that the letters need a reply and that this reply must be linked to the

information in the letter. Use examples to discuss the meaning of *consistent*.
- Write a reply to one of the letters on screen as an example. Invite the children to suggest how to open and close the letter, and discuss the content that needs to be included.
- Once everyone understands what they have to do, provide each child with a copy of photocopiable page 18 to complete.
- When they have finished, invite children to read their replies and discuss their consistency.

> **Differentiation**
> **For older/more confident learners:** Working in pairs, ask each child to write a letter for their partner, who can then write a reply.
> **For younger/less confident learners:** Work with the children on a short letter asking another member of staff to visit your classroom. Include a request for a reply.

Letter writing

> **Objective:** To select from different presentational features to suit particular writing purposes on paper and on screen.
> **What you need:** Copies of *Dear Greenpeace* and a selection of newspapers and magazines.

What to do
- Show the children one of the letters from Emily and one from Greenpeace. Point out how the lettering is more childlike in Emily's letter.
- Explore newspaper print, compare the fonts used and the size of lettering and draw the children's attention to large bold headlines. Point out how different fonts are used to highlight parts of the text.
- Type a formal letter – for example, to someone from the postal service asking him or her to come to your school and talk about how letters travel from sender to recipient. Display the letter on a

screen as you type, beginning with the address of the recipient. Decide on opening and closing words together and discuss essential content. Try out several different fonts and choose the one that the children think is most appropriate.
- When the children are satisfied with their letter, print it out and post it.
- Contrast this by asking the children to write an informal letter to a relative thanking them for a birthday present. Explain that, as this letter is informal, you would prefer them to handwrite it.

> **Differentiation**
> **For older/more confident learners:** Invite the children to type their own formal letters, experimenting with fonts and letter sizing.
> **For younger/less confident learners:** Ask the children to draw a picture of themselves and write *Thank you, from…* underneath. They can send their drawing to a recent visitor.

Plot, character and setting

All about Emily

● In these boxes, write down words and phrases to describe what Emily looks like and what is special about her character.

Appearance	Character

● Now use some of the words in the boxes to write sentences about Emily to build up a character profile.

_____

_____

_____

_____

_____

Illustration © 1991, Simon James.

Emily's feelings

● In the box under the picture, write a sentence about how Emily is feeling. Finish the sentences under the other small boxes about times and places when you have felt lonely. Draw a picture above each one to show what happened.

Emily is feeling…	**I felt lonely at school when…**
I felt lonely at home when…	**I felt lonely when I was…**

SECTION
4

When I grow up

● Read the questions below and write your answers underneath.
Be ready to read your sentences to the class and talk about what you
have written.

1. Emily is interested in all wildlife, especially whales. She also likes
music, reading and writing. **What are you interested in?**

_____

_____

_____

2. Emily reads books and writes letters to find out more about
her interests. **How can you find out more about the things you
are interested in?**

_____

_____

_____

3. Greenpeace suggests Emily might sail the oceans studying and
protecting whales when she grows up because she loves whales.
What would you like to do when you grow up?

_____

_____

_____

● On the other side of this sheet, draw a picture of yourself
as an adult doing something that interests you.

SECTION
4

Letter replies

- Read each letter carefully and then write a suitable reply.

---

65 Mountain Croft,
High Town,
PC1 2BD

Dear Flo,

I am writing to ask you and your Mum to come to tea at our house next Monday at 4 o'clock. Can you bring your new puppy with you? We would all like to see her. Is there anything special your puppy likes to eat?

Love,
Tom

Fir Tree Cottage,
Forest Lane,
Woodham,
DZ1 5GB

Dear Mr Jones,

I would like to make an appointment for a check-up at your surgery as I have toothache. Could you please let me know the date and time?

Yours sincerely,

Mary Thomas

---

24 Ambleside Road,
Laketown,
BL3 2PN

Dear Sir or Madam,

I am thinking of adopting one of your rescue dogs. Could you please send me an appointment to visit your Centre?

Could you also send me some information about how to care for a dog?

Yours sincerely,
Luke Davies

---

3 Green Street,
Millside,
Roseville

Dear Harry,

It was lovely to see you last weekend. I enjoyed making cakes with you. Would you like to come again this weekend and help me in the garden? What time will your Mum be able to bring you?

Lots of love,
Grandma xxx

SCHOLASTIC
www.scholastic.co.uk

Talk about it

Blue whales

Objective: To distinguish fiction and non-fiction texts and the different purposes for reading them.
What you need: Copies of *Dear Greenpeace*, books about whales such as *Rainbow Fish and the Big Blue Whale* by Marcus Pfister (North-South Books, fiction) and *Big Blue Whale* by Nicola Davies (Walker Books, non-fiction), access to websites such as www.nationalgeographic.com and www.enchantedlearning.com, photocopiable page 22 and writing materials.
Cross-curricular link: Science.

What to do
● Read *Dear Greenpeace* and discuss how Emily found out about blue whales. Ask: *What do we know about whales from reading the story?* (They live in salt water, always in oceans, eat shrimp-like creatures, are bigger than a pond and are migratory.)
● Discuss how to use books and websites to discover more about whales. Ask: *Which books do you think will give the most accurate information – fiction or non-fiction? Can you say why?*
● Divide the children into groups. Supply some groups with the chosen books and others with internet access. Provide writing materials and suggest that the children use the resources they have to note down facts about whales.
● Share the children's discoveries and compare the information sources.
● Display the enlarged copy of photocopiable page 22 and explain how to complete it. Provide each child with a copy to complete.

Differentiation
For older/more confident learners: Invite the children to compose their own missing word sentences. Display them on a screen to complete as a class.
For younger/less confident learners: Read titles from the non-fiction book selection with small groups of children so that whale facts can be reinforced.

Here comes the post!

Objective: To tell stories and describe incidents from their own experience in an audible voice.
What you need: Copies of *Dear Greenpeace* and examples of post brought in from home.
Cross-curricular link: PSHE.

What to do
● Read *Dear Greenpeace* with the class and discuss Emily's letters to Greenpeace. Ask: *Why did Emily write to Greenpeace? What did she want to know? Do you think she was happy with the replies she received? What else could she have done to find out information?* (She could have asked an expert, looked on a website or gone to the library to find books.)
● Explain to parents that you are discussing the purpose of writing letters and cards, and ask them to find interesting examples for their children to bring in and talk about. This could be a party invitation, birthday card or letter from a relative. (Check that they do not contain confidential material.)
● Invite the children and staff to talk about the importance of the post item they have brought in to the rest of the group. Encourage them to talk about the sender/recipient and the reason for the correspondence.
● Leave examples of post in the role-play area and provide writing tools and materials, along with forms from junk mail, for children to use in a home context.

Differentiation
For older/more confident learners: Ask the children to make up a story about receiving a special invitation.
For younger/less confident learners: Encourage the children to talk about any cards and parcels they received through the post on their birthday.

Talk about it

Making miniature scenes

> **Objective:** To listen to others in class, ask relevant questions and follow instructions.
> **What you need:** Copies of *Dear Greenpeace*, photocopiable page 23, cardboard box, paint, silver stars, curtain fabric, small bowl, plastic blue whale and a torch.
> **Cross-curricular links:** Design and technology, science.

What to do

● Explore the first image of Emily looking through her bedroom window. Ask: *What time of day is it? How can you tell? Can you describe the scene from Emily's point of view?*
● Invite groups of children to recreate this scene. Provide the suggested materials and discuss how to use them – for example, painting the box dark blue inside, shining the torch through a hole at the top, sticking silver stars on the sides, placing the whale in the bowl inside the box and closing the curtains. Provide assistance with techniques such as fastening fabric and making holes.
● Encourage the children to take turns to peep inside each completed box and describe the scene, pretending to be Emily.
● Display photocopiable page 23 and read the questions together. Explain that the aim of the sheet is to write instructions to make a miniature scene from *Dear Greenpeace* in a box.
● Provide each group with a copy to complete.
● Decide which set of instructions would be easiest to follow.

> **Differentiation**
> **For older/more confident learners:** Children can create miniature scenes from other books and write instruction sheets.
> **For younger/less confident learners:** Make the box beforehand and invite children to look through the curtains and share what they see.

There is a whale in my pond

> **Objectives:** To explain their views to others in a small group; to decide how to report the group's views to the class.
> **What you need:** Copies of *Dear Greenpeace*.

What to do

● Read *Dear Greenpeace* with the children and discuss Emily's possible reaction when she sees a whale in her pond. Write key words on the whiteboard and invite children to think of linked words – for example, Emily's thoughts about the whale – *huge, hurt, shiny, blue, smiling, lost, spurting*; Emily's feelings – *shock, excitement, curiosity, fear, happiness, love*; and Emily's actions – *feed, cuddle, stroke, get help, seek advice*. Leave these words on display.
● Suggest that the children work in groups to discuss Emily's reaction. Each group should choose one child to be Emily to report their collaborative view to the rest of the class. As they speak, the other groups will need to listen to what they are saying and ask questions.
● Give the groups time to think about how they are going to approach the activity, suggesting they make notes about Emily's reaction to help the reporter.
● After each group reporter has spoken, invite the other children to ask questions. If necessary, motivate them with a few of your own – for example, *Did you enjoy stroking the whale? Was it rough or smooth/warm or cold to touch?*

> **Differentiation**
> **For older/more confident learners:** Invite the groups to feed back about their impressions of the whole book, with each member reporting on a separate aspect.
> **For younger/less confident learners:** Work with a small group of children, helping them to verbalise their thoughts about what it would be like to find a whale in the garden.

Talk about it

Greenpeace

> **Objective:** To draw together ideas and information from across a text, using simple signposts in the text.
> **What you need:** Copies of *Dear Greenpeace* and access to the internet.
> **Cross-curricular link:** ICT.

What to do

● Read the book title: *Dear Greenpeace*. Ask: *Do you think Greenpeace is a person?* Discuss this possibility – after all, letters are usually written to one person. Point out contradictory clues in the book – for example, most letters to Emily include the word 'I', but one refers to 'us'.

● Look at the credits opposite the inside title page and point to the words 'Greenpeace UK'. Explain the word *organisation* and ask: *Now do you think Greenpeace is one person or an organisation?* Establish that Greenpeace is an organisation.

● Ask the children what they know about Greenpeace from the story. (It provides information about subjects such as the lifestyle of whales; it makes suggestions: *Perhaps it is a blue goldfish?*; it is concerned: *I am sorry to disappoint you*; it provides suggestions – for example, the adult Emily could protect whales with Greenpeace.)

● Return to the credits and read the sentence *The correspondence in this book is a work of fiction.* Ask the children: *Do you think the Greenpeace facts we have gathered are true? How can we make sure?* Look up the website address on this page, www.saveordelete.com, to obtain actual Greenpeace facts.

> **Differentiation**
> **For older/more confident learners:** Provide pictures and posters about endangered species for a role-play Greenpeace office.
> **For younger/less confident learners:** Pause to discuss how Greenpeace helped Emily as you read the letters in the book.

Imaginative creatures

> **Objective:** To explain ideas and processes using imaginative and adventurous vocabulary and non-verbal gestures to support communication.
> **What you need:** Copies of *Dear Greenpeace* and photocopiable page 24.

What to do

● Read *Dear Greenpeace* and ask the children if they think Emily's whale was real or in her imagination. Perhaps what she really saw was a big fish, a garden bush or just a dark shadow?

● Invite the children to imagine that they are looking out of their bedroom window during the night, just like Emily, and suggest that they see an unusual creature. Talk about what the creature might look like and how they might react when they see it. Support them with suggestions to enhance language and make it more imaginative and adventurous.

● Display the enlarged copy of photocopiable page 24 and read the questions together so that children understand what they need to do.

● Provide each child with a copy of the sheet to complete and encourage them to use imaginative language in their answers.

● Once the children have completed their sheets, ask them to take it in turns to describe their imagined creature to the rest of the class.

> **Differentiation**
> **For older/more confident learners:** Invite the children to make up a story about their encounter with their imagined creature and to read the stories aloud to the rest of the class.
> **For younger/less confident learners:** Ask the children to draw or paint a picture of an imagined creature they might see in the garden or park, and to think of a name for it. Help them to write the creature's name under the picture.

Talk about it

Blue whales

● Using the information you have discovered about whales, fill in the missing word in each sentence. The words you need are in the bottom box.

1. When a blue whale breathes out it blows ___ ___ ___ ___ ___ high up into the air.

2. Blue whales live in ___ ___ ___ ___ water.

3. Blue whales travel long distances so they are called

___ ___ ___ ___ ___ ___ ___ ___ ___ .

4. Blue whales are the largest mammals on

our ___ ___ ___ ___ ___ ___ .

5. Blue whales eat small shrimp-like creatures

called ___ ___ ___ ___ ___ .

6. Blue whales live in groups called ___ ___ ___ ___ with other whales.

| migratory | planet | salt | krill | pods | water |

Illustration © 2009, Theresa Tibbetts/Beehive Illustrations.

Talk about it

Making miniature scenes

● Answer these questions to explain how you made your miniature scene.

1. What did you need to make the scene?

_____

_____

2. How did you create the effect of light from a street lamp?

_____

_____

3. How did you make the pond?

_____

_____

4. What else did you put in the garden?

_____

_____

5. What did you like best about your scene?

_____

_____

Imaginative creatures

● Picture your imaginary creature. Read each question carefully and write down your answers. Draw your creature in the final box.

Where did you see your creature?	How big is your creature?
What is special about your creature?	What is your creature called?
What was your creature doing?	Draw a picture of your creature here:

SCHOLASTIC
www.scholastic.co.uk

READ & RESPOND: Activities based on Dear Greenpeace

Get writing

Breakfast time

> **Objective:** To group written sentences together in chunks of meaning or subject.
> **What you need:** Copies of *Dear Greenpeace* and photocopiable page 28.
> **Cross-curricular link:** PSHE.

What to do

● Read *Dear Greenpeace* with the children and encourage close observation of the illustration of Emily's family having breakfast. Ask questions such as: *Who do we know is at the table? Can we tell who is reading the paper? Who might it be? What is the family eating? Is anyone having a drink? Do you think it is hot or cold? What is the baby doing?*

● Encourage the children to compare this image with their own breakfast-time experiences. Ask: *Who is usually there at breakfast time? What do they eat? Do they talk or read while they are eating?*

● Display an enlarged copy of photocopiable page 28 and explain that it will help the children to compare Emily's breakfast time with their own. Discuss what they enjoy eating and who they have breakfast with to help them to think about different aspects of breakfast time.

● Hand out sheets for the children to complete.

● When they have finished, discuss the children's work and compare their experiences with Emily's.

> **Differentiation**
> **For older/more confident learners:** Suggest that children write sentences about themselves under a series of headings, such as 'My appearance', 'My family', 'My friends' and 'My interests'.
> **For younger/less confident learners:** Set up a role-play breakfast time and encourage discussion about home experiences, before supporting children as they write simple linked sentences.

Storybook letters

> **Objectives:** To choose what to write about independently; to make a plan and follow it through.
> **What you need:** Copies of *Dear Greenpeace*, photocopiable page 29, six cardboard boxes, scissors, envelopes, glue sticks and writing materials.

What to do

● Transform the cardboard boxes into postboxes by sticking on the labels from photocopiable page 29.

● Explore the cover of *Dear Greenpeace* with the children. Ask: *What can we see on the cover that you can find on a letter?* (Stamp and postmark.)

● Display an enlarged copy of photocopiable page 29 and read the addresses together. Ask: *What do you notice about the addresses?* (They are fictitious addresses for storybook characters.)

● Discuss who these characters might receive letters from, and the possible content.

● Give each group of six children scissors, glue sticks, envelopes and writing materials and a copy of photocopiable page 29. Ask them to cut out the labels, share them randomly, stick each one to an envelope and draw on a stamp and postmark.

● Invite the children to compose a letter to their character, put it in the envelope and post it in the relevant postbox.

● Re-assemble the class and take on a character's role, emptying his/her postbox and reading the letters aloud. Ask: *What were the letters about? Which one did you like best? Can you say why?*

> **Differentiation**
> **For older/more confident learners:** Ask the children to choose different characters, invent addresses and then write letters to them.
> **For younger/less confident learners:** Encourage the children to draw a picture instead of writing a letter, and to write their names underneath.

Get writing

Answers to questions

Objective: To compose and write sentences independently to communicate meaning.
What you need: Copies of *Dear Greenpeace*, writing materials and access to the internet.
Cross-curricular links: PSHE and ICT.

What to do

● Read *Dear Greenpeace* with the class and discuss why Emily wrote to this organisation. (Because it works with endangered species and knows all about whales.)
● Invite the children to suggest an environmental issue that interests or concerns them – for example, how wild animals can be endangered by people dropping rubbish.
● Choose a favourite topic together and do a web search to decide on the sort of organisations to contact for information.
● Collect a list of appropriate websites – for example, www.countrysideaccess.gov.uk – and look for contact details. (If a site gives an email rather than a postal address, children can compose a letter and send it as an email.)
● Ask the children to write questions on the whiteboard – for example, *How is rubbish a danger to wildlife?* Note the most appropriate organisation for answering each question.
● Invite the children to work in groups to compose a letter to one of the chosen organisations.
● Bring the class together to share and modify their letters. Post or send them and await replies.

Differentiation
For older/more confident learners: Invite the children to write simple instruction sheets relating to an environmental project – for example, how to make a nesting box or bird cake.
For younger/less confident learners: Explore reference books about an environmental topic together. Ask the children to draw pictures and write simple sentences about facts they have discovered.

Arthur's journey

Objective: To use planning to establish clear sections for writing.
What you need: Copies of *Dear Greenpeace* and photocopiable page 30.

What to do

● Read *Dear Greenpeace* and make sure that the children understand key story elements, such as plot, character and setting by asking, for example: *Where does the story take place? Who is the main character? Who else is in the story? What happens?*
● Focus on what happens to Arthur. Ask: *Where was Arthur at the beginning of the story? Where was he at the end? Do we know how he got from the pond to the ocean?*
● Suggest that children make up stories about Arthur's journey.
● Display an enlarged copy of photocopiable page 30 and explain to the children that the page is divided into sections to help them to plan the beginning, middle and end of their stories. Read the questions together.
● Provide each child with a copy of the sheet and ask them to make notes about their story's setting, characters and plot.
● Once they have completed their notes, discuss storybook language such as *In the beginning, Once upon a time, After that, By and by, Happily ever after* and *In the end*. Ask the children to write out their stories in full.

Differentiation
For older/more confident learners: Invite pairs of children to take turns to read their stories while the other listens and makes helpful comments.
For younger/less confident learners: Ask the children to draw pictures to tell their story, with a short sentence under each one describing the action.

Get writing

Web designers

> **Objective:** To work effectively in groups by ensuring that each group member takes a turn challenging, supporting and moving on.
> **What you need:** Copies of *Dear Greenpeace*, internet access, writing/art materials and large sheets of card.
> **Cross-curricular link:** ICT.

What to do
● Read *Dear Greenpeace* and discuss the role the organisation plays in the story.
● Search for websites of organisations that work to protect whales – for example, www.savethewhales.org and www.IFAW.org. Talk about how they design their home pages and use images, lettering, animation and graphics.
● Suggest that the children invent their own whale-related organisation – for example, 'We love whales' – and design a home web page.
● On the whiteboard, invite children to write down things that they liked on the websites explored – images, videos, children's links and so on. Ask: *Which of these would you put on your website? What else would you include?*
● Divide the class into groups and provide sheets of card and writing and art materials. Suggest that each group chooses a name for their organisation and draws out a design for their web page on the card. Ask them to allocate roles for each member of the group, such as finding or drawing images, writing words and adding special effects using art materials.
● Display the finished posters for discussion.

> **Differentiation**
> **For older/more confident learners:** Invite the children to create individual mini-posters about environmental issues.
> **For younger/less confident learners:** Ask the children to draw a large picture of a whale and use their drawings in a wall display about saving whales.

Book review

> **Objective:** To explain their reactions to texts, commenting on important aspects.
> **What you need:** Copies of *Dear Greenpeace* and a selection of reviews of the children's favourite books (look on book covers or search the internet).

What to do
● Read *Dear Greenpeace* and invite the children to comment on the book's layout and illustrations. Focus on the way the story is presented in the form of letters. Ask: *Is this effective?*
● Explain the purpose of a book review and read examples of reviews of favourite books, focusing on how the information is presented. Suggest that the children write a *Dear Greenpeace* review.
● Discuss the characters in the book. Ask: *Do you think Emily is a suitable main character? Can you give reasons why? Do we have enough information about the baby, Dad and Arthur or would the story work better with more detail?*
● Now talk about the book's setting. Ask: *Where does most of the story take place? Do you like stories set in a character's home or do you prefer more adventurous places?*
● Ask the children what they liked and disliked about the story events. Ask: *Were you satisfied with the ending? Do you think the author could have included more action involving Arthur or is it better left to our imaginations?*
● Encourage the children to make notes under the headings *Characters, Setting* and *Events* before writing their reviews out in full.

> **Differentiation**
> **For older/more confident learners:** Invite the children to choose another story to write a review about, using the same approach.
> **For younger/less confident learners:** Ask the children what they liked best about the book and invite them to draw a picture that shows this. Support them by writing an accompanying sentence.

Get writing

Breakfast time

● Use this sheet to compare your breakfast time with Emily's. Look at the picture of Emily having breakfast and answer the questions.

Who is Emily with?

_____

What is everyone eating?

_____

What else is happening?

_____

● Below, draw a picture of you having breakfast and answer the questions.

Who is with you?

_____

What is everyone eating?

_____

_____

What else is happening?

_____

_____

Get writing

Storybook letters

● The labels below are addressed to different storybook characters. Cut them out and stick each one onto an envelope.

Little Red Riding Hood,
The Cottage,
Fir Tree Lane,
Woodside

The Ugly Troll,
The Wooden Bridge,
Meadowside,
Green Pastures

Arthur, the Blue Whale,
Emily's Pond,
The Back Garden,
4 Sunshine Road,
Hope Town

The Giant,
The Castle,
Beanstalk Top,
Cloudland

The Wild Things,
High Moonlit Path,
Deep, Dark Forest,
Faraway Land

The Three Little Pigs,
Chimney House,
Brick Lane,
Story Town

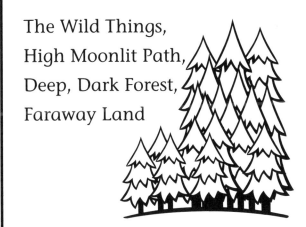

Get writing

Arthur's journey

- Plan a story about Arthur's journey from the pond to the ocean.

Main characters and setting

Beginning
- Where is Arthur at the beginning of the story and why does he leave Emily's pond?

Middle
- What happens to Arthur after he leaves the pond?
  - Where does he go? • Who does he meet?

End
- How does the story end?

READ & RESPOND: Activities based on *Dear Greenpeace*

Assessment

Assessment advice

Ongoing formative assessments of individual achievements and progress in literacy are an essential component of the planning and assessment cycle. They help teachers to make valuable judgements about a child's progress towards specific learning targets, and also to ensure that future learning activities are planned at an appropriate level. Assessment outcomes are invaluable in determining new individual targets. Reports and assessments should be based on clear evidence arising from observations and examples of actual work completed.

Formative assessments build up gradually and should be created from a variety of sources, such as observations, contributions to classroom discussions, peer group interaction and analysis of children's practical work. The importance of peer- and self-assessment should not be overlooked. All of the activities in this book can be assessed using a combination of these methods.

Each activity has a clear assessable learning objective which represents what a child should know, or be able to do, by the end of that activity. Informing children of these objectives before an activity begins is essential in order to help them to recognise their involvement in their own learning. Likewise, at the end of each activity there should be a time for reflection when children can revisit the learning objective and discuss whether or not they feel they have achieved it. This helps them to understand the significance of assessment in planning the next steps in learning.

You can use the assessment activity on photocopiable page 32 as part of a record of individual progress. It is also a useful tool for assessing a child's letter-writing ability.

Letter planning

> **Assessment focus:** To draw on knowledge and experience of texts in deciding and planning what and how to write.
> **What you need:** A copy of *Dear Greenpeace*, photocopiable page 32, examples of different types of letters and letter-writing resources.

What to do

● Read *Dear Greenpeace* with the children and discuss the contrasting letters written by Emily and Greenpeace.

● Explore the selection of letters together and talk about experiences of receiving letters at home.

● Remind the children of the words *formal* and *informal* and discuss the differences between the two styles, showing examples.

● Explain that a letter, like a story, has a beginning, middle and end. Write *Dear...* on the whiteboard, and a selection of formal and informal closing words such as *Yours sincerely, Yours faithfully, Love* and *Best wishes*.

● Suggest that the children compose a formal or informal letter to someone.

● Display the enlarged copy of photocopiable page 32 and explain to the children that this will help them plan their letter. Read the page aloud and ask questions to ensure that everyone understands what is expected of them. Provide each child with a copy of the sheet to use to write a letter plan.

● As the children are writing, interact with individuals to support their ideas. Focus on appropriate opening and closing words and the information they wish to include.

● Invite the children to write out their letters in full, referring to their written plans.

Assessment

Letter planning

- Use this sheet to plan your letter.

- Is your letter formal or informal?

- What is the address of the person you are writing to?

Beginning

- Who is your letter to? How are you going to begin your letter?

Middle

- What is the letter about? What questions will you be asking?

End

- Make a note of words you could use to end your letter.

Illustration © 1991, Simon James.